ARTIST TRANSCRIPTIONS
SAXOPHONE

THE MINDI ABAIR Collection

T0080116

Cover photo by Reisig and Taylor, courtesy of Peak/Concord Records
Interior photo by Jeff Bender

ISBN 978-1-4234-8018-1

HAL•LEONARD®
CORPORATION
7777 W. BLUEMOUND RD. P.O. BOX 13819 MILWAUKEE, WI 53213

For all works contained herein:
Unauthorized copying, arranging, adapting, recording, Internet posting, public
performance, or other distribution of the printed music in this publication is an
infringement of copyright. Infringers are liable under the law.

Visit Hal Leonard Online at
www.halleonard.com

Biography

Saxophonist/Singer/Songwriter Mindi Abair has not only set sonic trends, but has broken all the boundaries as she continues to define the less traditional future of jazz. Her own brand of pop-meets-jazz adds a refreshingly unique voice to an exciting new generation of crossover artists who are, like her, powerful instrumentalists as well as thought-provoking singer/songwriters. This Florida-raised, Los Angeles-based performer's unique hybrid sound—a mix of cool vulnerability and utter conviction—have brought her to the top of her game. She tours with her own band to sold out audiences worldwide, hosts a popular nationally syndicated radio show "Chill with Mindi Abair", and the list of artists she has toured or recorded with are a testament to her talent. They include the Backstreet Boys, Duran Duran, Mandy Moore, Josh Groban, Adam Sandler, Keb' Mo', Lalah Hathaway, Lee Ritenour, Teena Marie, John Tesh, Bobby Lyle, Jeff Golub, Jonathan Butler, Peter White and Rick Braun.

When asked about their childhoods and musical influences, many artists look back fondly on a certain album or song they heard, or certain moment of epiphany where their future came clear. "Not me," says Abair, a St. Petersburg, Florida native who spent much of her early life on the road with her father's band. "Between watching my father onstage and spending time with my grandmother, who was an opera singer, music was always around me. My parents gave in to my constant banging on the piano with lessons at age five, and when I was able to choose a band instrument in fourth grade, I copied my father and went straight for the saxophone. Music was always my normal. I never considered doing anything else. And by the time someone told me it was odd for a girl to play an instrument for a living, thankfully it was too late."

Her 2003 debut CD, *It Just Happens That Way*, debuted in the Top 5 on the *Billboard* Contemporary Jazz Chart and remained in the Top 10 for 19 consecutive weeks. *Billboard* magazine named *It Just Happens That Way* one of the top 10 Contemporary Jazz CDs of the year. Her hit single "Lucy's" was #1 on R&R for a record-breaking eight weeks and Abair was hailed for leading a new movement in contemporary music. Her 2004 release *Come As You Are* debuted at #5 on the

Billboard Contemporary Jazz charts. Her 2006 release *Life Less Ordinary* debuted at #1 on the *Billboard* Contemporary Jazz Chart and remained in the Top 20 for 45 weeks. Her songs "True Blue" and "Bloom" hit #1 on R&R. Her 2008 release *Stars* broke the usual genre barriers, with her single "Stars" charting #29 Adult Contemporary R&R simultaneously with her single "Smile" hitting Top 10 on the R&R Jazz Airplay charts.

Mindi Abair has opened for Josh Groban, was a featured performer in the "Women in Jazz" feature at the Grammys, and has appeared up on Panasonic's Jumbotron in Times Square, the "Drew Carey Show," HGTV, "Emeril Live," and onstage with Adam Sandler on his HBO Special and 2008's MTV Movie Awards, backing him up for his Lifetime Achievement Award. Her songs have been featured on everything from the Robin Williams/Mandy Moore movie *License to Wed* to Aaron Spelling's hit "Summerland." Mindi's recording of her original Christmas song "I Can't Wait for Christmas" was featured in 2005 on the Bath & Body Works and Pier One Christmas CDs, selling almost one million copies.

Critical raves have come from the press and artists alike. Josh Groban has commented: "I was a fan the moment I saw a tape of one of her concerts. Her ability to connect with the crowd and appeal to jazz fans as well as those who aren't as familiar with her makes her such an exciting artist, and I was thrilled to have her as a guest on my tour." *JAZZIZ* magazine said "Mindi Abair is #1 for her original sound, perfect melodies, grooves and overall sense of fun." Blues giant Keb' Mo' takes it deeper: "She speaks to all of our souls. Do yourself a favor and check out Mindi Abair's music. You'll be happy you did."

Bloom

Alto Sax

Composed by
Mindi Abair and Matthew Hager

Copyright © 2006 UNIVERSAL MUSIC CORP., NOT MORE SAXOPHONE MUSIC
and PENNY FARTHING MUSIC o/b/o 76 STEPS MUSIC c/o THE BICYCLE MUSIC COMPANY
All Rights for NOT MORE SAXOPHONE MUSIC Controlled and Administered by UNIVERSAL MUSIC CORP.
All Rights Reserved   Used by Permission

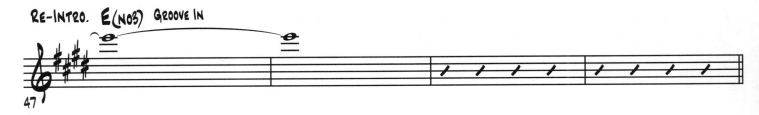

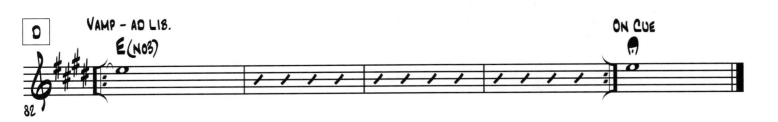

Come As You Are

Alto Sax

Composed by
Mindi Abair and Matthew Hager

Copyright © 2004 UNIVERSAL MUSIC CORP., NOT MORE SAXOPHONE MUSIC
and PENNY FARTHING MUSIC o/b/o 76 STEPS MUSIC c/o THE BICYCLE MUSIC COMPANY
All Rights for NOT MORE SAXOPHONE MUSIC Controlled and Administered by UNIVERSAL MUSIC CORP.
All Rights Reserved   Used by Permission

10

SAX ONLY

Every Time

Soprano Sax

Words and music by
Mindi Abair and Matthew Hager

Copyright © 2004 UNIVERSAL MUSIC CORP., NOT MORE SAXOPHONE MUSIC
and PENNY FARTHING MUSIC o/b/o 76 STEPS MUSIC c/o THE BICYCLE MUSIC COMPANY
All Rights for NOT MORE SAXOPHONE MUSIC Controlled and Administered by UNIVERSAL MUSIC CORP.
All Rights Reserved   Used by Permission

EV-'RY TIME— I— SEE— YOUR FACE,— EV-'RY SMILE,— EV-'RY WARM— EM-BRACE,—

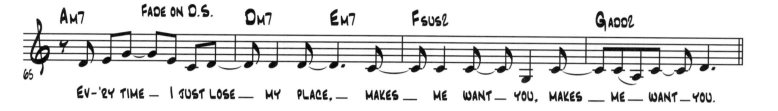

EV-'RY TIME— I JUST LOSE— MY PLACE,— MAKES— ME WANT— YOU, MAKES— ME— WANT— YOU.

If I CALLED— YOUR NAME,— WOULD YOU FEEL— THE SAME?—

Flirt

Soprano Sax

Composed by
Mindi Abair and Matthew Hager

Copyright © 2003 UNIVERSAL MUSIC CORP., NOT MORE SAXOPHONE MUSIC
and PENNY FARTHING MUSIC o/b/o 76 STEPS MUSIC c/o THE BICYCLE MUSIC COMPANY
All Rights for NOT MORE SAXOPHONE MUSIC Controlled and Administered by UNIVERSAL MUSIC CORP.
All Rights Reserved   Used by Permission

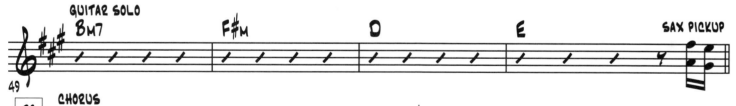

The Joint

Alto Sax

Composed By
Mindi Abair and Matthew Hager

Copyright © 2006 UNIVERSAL MUSIC CORP., NOT MORE SAXOPHONE MUSIC
and PENNY FARTHING MUSIC o/b/o 76 STEPS MUSIC c/o THE BICYCLE MUSIC COMPANY
All Rights for NOT MORE SAXOPHONE MUSIC Controlled and Administered by UNIVERSAL MUSIC CORP.
All Rights Reserved   Used by Permission

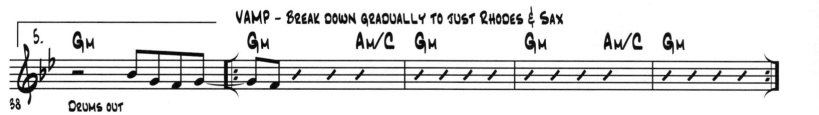

Lucy's

Alto Sax

Composed by
Mindi Abair and Matthew Hager

Copyright © 2003 UNIVERSAL MUSIC CORP., NOT MORE SAXOPHONE MUSIC
and PENNY FARTHING MUSIC o/b/o 76 STEPS MUSIC c/o THE BICYCLE MUSIC COMPANY
All Rights for NOT MORE SAXOPHONE MUSIC Controlled and Administered by UNIVERSAL MUSIC CORP.
All Rights Reserved   Used by Permission

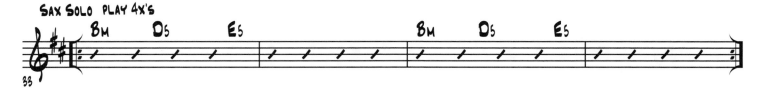

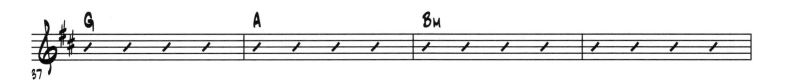

Make A Wish

Alto Sax

Composed by
Mindi Abair and Tyrone Stevens

Copyright © 2004 UNIVERSAL MUSIC CORP., NOT MORE SAXOPHONE MUSIC, WB MUSIC CORP. and SOBBLE DEBOP
All Rights for NOT MORE SAXOPHONE MUSIC Controlled and Administered by UNIVERSAL MUSIC CORP.
All Rights for SOBBLE DEBOP Administered by WB MUSIC CORP.
All Rights Reserved   Used by Permission

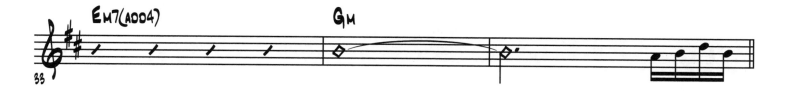

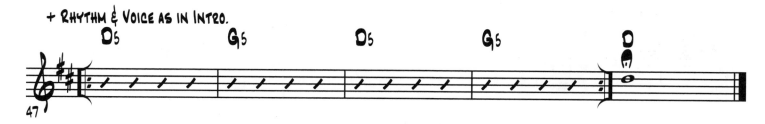

Remember

Alto Sax

Composed by
Mindi Abair and Matthew Hager

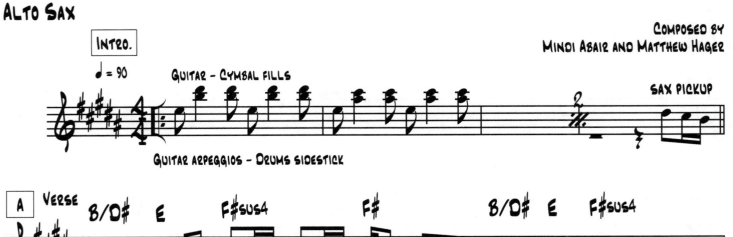

Copyright © 2003 UNIVERSAL MUSIC CORP., NOT MORE SAXOPHONE MUSIC, WB MUSIC CORP. and SOBBLE DEBOP
All Rights for NOT MORE SAXOPHONE MUSIC Controlled and Administered by UNIVERSAL MUSIC CORP.
All Rights for SOBBLE DEBOP Administered by WB MUSIC CORP.
All Rights Reserved   Used by Permission

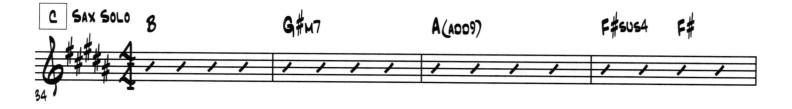

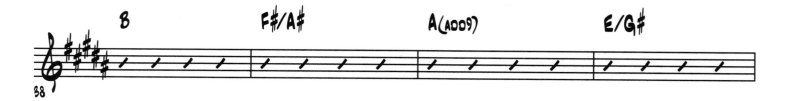

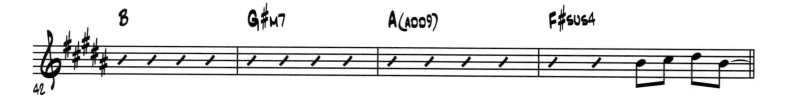

Save The Last Dance

Soprano Sax

Composed by
Mindi Abair and Tyrone Stevens

Copyright © 2003 UNIVERSAL MUSIC CORP., NOT MORE SAXOPHONE MUSIC, WB MUSIC CORP. and SOBBLE DEBOP
All Rights for NOT MORE SAXOPHONE MUSIC Controlled and Administered by UNIVERSAL MUSIC CORP.
All Rights for SOBBLE DEBOP Administered by WB MUSIC CORP.
All Rights Reserved   Used by Permission

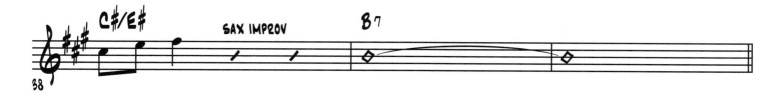

Rain

Alto Sax

Composed by
Mindi Abair and Matthew Hager

Copyright © 2006 UNIVERSAL MUSIC CORP., NOT MORE SAXOPHONE MUSIC
and PENNY FARTHING MUSIC o/b/o 76 STEPS MUSIC c/o THE BICYCLE MUSIC COMPANY
All Rights for NOT MORE SAXOPHONE MUSIC Controlled and Administered by UNIVERSAL MUSIC CORP.
All Rights Reserved   Used by Permission

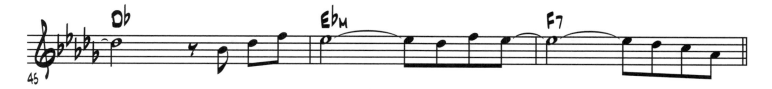

Smile

Alto Sax

Composed by
Mindi Abair and Matthew Hager

Copyright © 2008 UNIVERSAL MUSIC CORP., NOT MORE SAXOPHONE MUSIC
and PENNY FARTHING MUSIC o/b/o 76 STEPS MUSIC c/o THE BICYCLE MUSIC COMPANY
All Rights for NOT MORE SAXOPHONE MUSIC Controlled and Administered by UNIVERSAL MUSIC CORP.
All Rights Reserved   Used by Permission

30

Stars

Soprano Sax

Words and Music by
Mindi Abair and Matthew Hager

Copyright © 2006, 2008 UNIVERSAL MUSIC CORP., NOT MORE SAXOPHONE MUSIC
and PENNY FARTHING MUSIC o/b/o 76 STEPS MUSIC c/o THE BICYCLE MUSIC COMPANY
All Rights for NOT MORE SAXOPHONE MUSIC Controlled and Administered by UNIVERSAL MUSIC CORP.
All Rights Reserved   Used by Permission

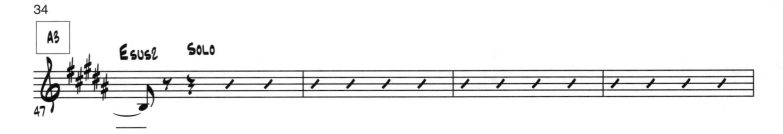

True Blue

Alto Sax

Composed by
Mindi Abair and Matthew Hager

Copyright © 2006 UNIVERSAL MUSIC CORP., NOT MORE SAXOPHONE MUSIC
and PENNY FARTHING MUSIC o/b/o 76 STEPS MUSIC c/o THE BICYCLE MUSIC COMPANY
All Rights for NOT MORE SAXOPHONE MUSIC Controlled and Administered by UNIVERSAL MUSIC CORP.
All Rights Reserved   Used by Permission

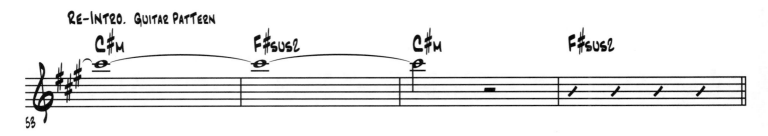

26 Hemenway

Alto Sax

Composed by
Mindi Abair and Russell Ferrante

Copyright © 2004 UNIVERSAL MUSIC CORP., NOT MORE SAXOPHONE MUSIC and TEETH MUSIC
All Rights for NOT MORE SAXOPHONE MUSIC Controlled and Administered by UNIVERSAL MUSIC CORP.
All Rights Reserved   Used by Permission